C000163889

Progressive
CHROMATIC HARMONICA

by
Peter Gelling

Published by
KOALA MUSIC PUBLICATIONS™

PROGRESSIVE CHROMATIC HARMONICA
by Peter Gelling
ISBN: 978-1-86469-079-8
Order Code: 69079

Visit our Website
www.learntoplaymusic.com

Contact us via email
info@learntoplaymusic.com

Like us on Facebook
www.facebook.com/LearnToPlayMusic

Follow us on Twitter
twitter.com/LTPMusic

View our YouTube Channel
www.youtube.com/learntoplaymusiccom

LTP LearnToPlayMusic™
RC-RPPP-C

CONTENTS

INTRODUCTION

Progressive Chromatic Harmonica assumes you have no prior knowledge of chromatic harmonica playing, but it will be to your advantage if you have played the diatonic harmonica (e.g. Folk or Blues harmonica) or another musical instrument. This book can take you from **beginner to professional level on the chromatic harp**. In the course of the book you will learn **all the essential techniques of chromatic harmonica playing** along with how to read music, how to improvise and how to analyze music and musical forms. By the end of the book you will be ready to play in a band, understand improvisation and be competent in a variety of musical styles.

All harmonica players should know all of the information contained in this book.

The best and fastest way to learn is to use this book in conjunction with:
1. Buying sheet music and song books of your favorite recording artists and learning to play their songs. By learning songs, you will begin to build a repertoire and always have something to play in jam sessions.
2. Practicing and playing with other musicians. You will be surprised how good a basic drums/bass/guitar/harmonica or simply harmonica and guitar combination can sound even when playing easy music.
3. Learning by listening to your favorite recordings. Start a collection of albums of players you admire or wish to emulate. Try playing along with one of them for a short time each day. Most of the great harmonica players have learned a lot of their music this way.

Also in the early stages it is helpful to have the guidance of an experienced teacher. This will also help you keep to a schedule and obtain weekly goals. To help you develop a good sense of time it is recommended that you **always** practice with a metronome or drum machine.

USING THE AUDIO

It's recommended that you use the accompanying audio available (see the front of this book for more details). The book explains the techniques to use, while the audio lets you hear how each example should sound when played correctly.

 ◄——— This icon with a number indicates that a recorded example is available.

Practice the examples on your own, playing slowly at first. Then try playing with a metronome set to a slow tempo, until you can play the example evenly and without stopping. Gradually increase the tempo as you become more confident and then you can try playing along with the recordings.

THE CHROMATIC HARMONICA

The chromatic harmonica is bigger than the diatonic (Folk or Blues harmonica) and has a lot more notes available on it. It is possible to play in **all keys** on the chromatic harmonica by using the **slide**, which is depressed (pushed in) to create extra notes. The most common chromatic harmonica has **12** holes and covers a range of three octaves. Although there are other keys, the **C** chromatic harmonica is the most common and is the one used in this book.

There are **two rows of holes** on the chromatic harmonica. The **top** row contains **all the natural notes**. The bottom row is blocked unless you press in the slide. When you depress the slide, it opens the bottom row which contains all the sharps and flats and at the same time blocks off the top row of notes. The use of the slide gives you **24** holes instead of 12.

Slide

HOLDING THE CHROMATIC HARMONICA

The left hand position for holding the chromatic harmonica is identical to that of the diatonic, but there are two possible positions for the right hand. Some players prefer to control the slide with their index finger and use the position in the photo on the left. Others prefer to control the slide with their thumb and use the position in the photo on the right. Experiment with both positions and use whichever is most comfortable.

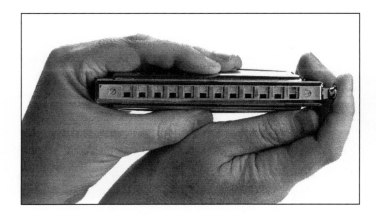

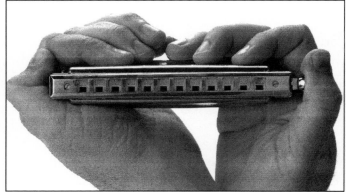

As mentioned above, by using the slide you double the number of notes available on the chromatic harmonica. The following example demonstrates the four notes available from hole number **1**. The first note is an exhale note without the slide depressed (pushed in). This is followed by a different exhale note on hole 1 created by pushing in the slide. Listen to the recording and then try it yourself.

 1   Using the Slide on hole number 1

UNDERSTANDING MUSIC

Although it is possible to play the harmonica totally by ear, you can get a lot further by learning to read and understand written music. Since it is the brain which issues the information for playing, it is most important to train the brain to recognize written notes as well as sounds and to build up a bank of knowledge which makes it easier to understand the whole process of making music. This has the added benefit of helping you to relate to what other musicians are playing and understanding the way a song's melody and its accompaniment work together, as well as making it easier to understand the sheet music of any song you wish to learn.

STANDARD MUSIC NOTATION

The musical alphabet consists of **7** letters:

A B C D E F G

Music is written on a **STAFF**, which consists of 5 parallel lines. Notes are written on these lines and in the spaces between them.

MUSIC STAFF

THE TREBLE or **'G' CLEF** is placed at the beginning of each staff line. This clef indicates the position of the note G.

The **head** of a note indicates its position, on the staff, e.g.:

When the note head is below the middle staff line the stem points upward and when the head is above the middle line the stem points downward. A note placed on the middle line (**B**) can have its stem pointing either up or down.

LEARNING THE NOTES ON THE STAFF

To remember the notes on the lines of the staff, say:
Every **G**ood **B**oy **D**eserves **F**ruit.

The notes in the spaces spell:
F A C E

Extra notes can be added above or below the staff using short lines, called **LEDGER LINES**.

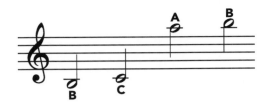

Bar lines are drawn across the staff, dividing the music into sections called **Bars** or **Measures**. A **Final bar line** signifies the end of the music.

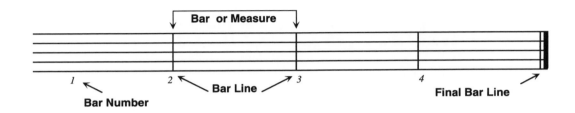

THE QUARTER NOTE

This is a **quarter note**. It lasts for **one** beat or count.

Count: **1**

THE FOUR FOUR TIME SIGNATURE

These two numbers are called the **four four time signature**.
They are placed after the treble clef.
The 4/4 time signature tells you there are four beats in each bar.
There are **four** quarter notes in one bar of music in 4/4 time.

KEEPING TIME

One of the most important aspects of playing any instrument is keeping a strong, even sense of time while you play. This is best developed by counting the rhythms in the music. Before you play the scale on the following page, count **1 2 3 4 1 2 3 4** several times to get a feel for the rhythm. As you play the example, count mentally as you play and tap your foot to help you keep time. To be sure you develop a good sense of time right from the beginning, it is recommended that you **always practice with a metronome or drum machine**. This is discussed further on page 9. Each example on the recording begins with a drum beat intro. Count along with these beats to help you establish the right tempo (speed) for each example.

NOTES ON THE CHROMATIC HARMONICA

The following diagram shows the names of all of the natural notes on the **C** Chromatic harmonica. These are the notes on the **top row** of holes. Without the slide pushed in, all the holes on the bottom row are blocked off. Using these notes is discussed in lesson 3. For now, you can ignore them and just learn the notes on the top row.

TOP ROW OF NOTES

			Same note				Same note				
Exhale			↘ ↙				↘ ↙				
C	E	G	C C	E	G	C C	E	G	C
1	**2**	**3**	**4**	**5**	**6**	**7**	**8**	**9**	**10**	**11**	**12**
D	F	A	B	D	F	A	B	D	F	A	B
Inhale											

THE C MAJOR SCALE

A **major scale** is a group of eight notes that produces the familiar sound:

Do Re Mi Fa So La Ti Do

Shown below are the notes of the **C** major scale.

C   D   E   F   G   A   B   C

The names of the first and last notes of a major scale are always the same. In the C major scale, the distance from the first **C** to the other **C** note is **one octave** (eight notes).

BREATHING INDICATORS

On the harmonica, some notes are produced by breathing out, while others are produced by breathing in. An **exhale** breath is indicated by the letter **e** and an **inhale** breath is indicated by the letter **i**. The notation below shows one octave of the **C** major scale played in quarter notes. The letters **e** and **i** indicate the correct breathing. The numbers under the breathing letters indicate the holes on the harmonica. Notice that the higher C can be played on both holes **4 and 5**.

  2   C Major Scale

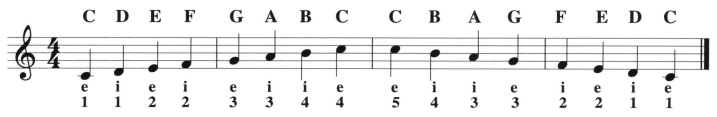

NOTE VALUES

Table of Notes · **Note Rest**

Note: When counting, the following symbols are pronounced thus:

+ = 'an'
e = 'ee'
a = 'uh'
r = 'er'

UNDERSTANDING NOTE VALUES

The table of notes shows every note type you are likely to encounter, with the corresponding rests for each in the next column (note rests). Here are a few points to help you understand note values:

1. Tempo (beats per minute) dictates the speed of a piece of music. If the tempo is ♩= 60, one quarter note is being played every second. If the time signature is $\frac{4}{4}$, the information contained within one bar must run for the same duration as four quarter notes (or four seconds). Any note type(s) can be used within the bar. Therefore, note values are like fractions, dividing the amount of notes being played over a specific time period into different amounts. At a fixed tempo, the greater the number of notes per bar, the greater the speed at which they are played.

2. In $\frac{4}{4}$ time, the digits 1-4 and the sounds **e, + , a , r** are used when counting, to signify fractional divisions of the bar.

3. Wherever possible, notes are grouped together to make reading easier e.g. sixteenth notes are grouped together in fours rather than written individually.

THE METRONOME

A metronome is a mechanical or electronic device that emits a sound to indicate a specific tempo. The tempo (beats per minute) is adjustable.

The metronome has four functions:

1. It allows you to find an exact tempo.
2. It acts as a control for your timing so that you don't rush or slow down during your playing.
3. It indicates improvements which might otherwise go unnoticed.
4. It shows you the level and boundaries of your technique.

Using the metronome:

1. Set the metronome at a comfortable tempo and play the specific exercise through 20 times.

2. Reset the metronome 4-8 beats faster and again, play the exercise 20 times.

3. Repeat this process until you reach a tempo where you begin to struggle and tense up. Reset the metronome 4-8 beats slower and again, play the exercise 20 times.

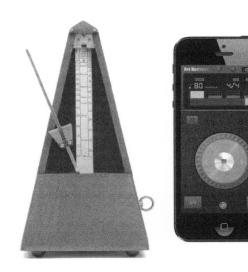

You can purchase a metronome from a music instrument store or download a metronome app to your smartphone or tablet. There are many paid and free app options and we recommend Pro Metronome (Android/ iOS) or The Metronome by Soundbrenner (Android/ iOS).

4. Whenever you feel tense repeat step 3. Remember, the way to achieve speed is to remain relaxed and practice precisely. Practicing when you're tense will only teach you how to be tense, and in the long term may cause physical damage.

DEVELOPING YOUR MUSIC READING

Because it is possible to play in all keys on the chromatic harmonica, it is possible to play a lot of music which could not be played on a diatonic harmonica. Some music can be learned simply by listening to recordings and imitating what you hear. However, recordings only began in the 20th century and there is a whole world of great music written before the 20th century which is unavailable to you if you can't read music.

Even where there are recordings, as music becomes more complex it is harder to learn by ear. If you can read music well, you can often learn a new piece of music in a very short time. This ability allows musicians to play easily with a new group they have never played with before by the use of **"charts"** which contain the melody and chord changes to songs. If you intend to play Jazz or Classical music, it is essential to develop your ability to read and understand music in all keys.

The first step in developing this ability is learning to read scales and simple tunes without the aid of inhale and exhale or hole number markings. Shown below is the notation for a C major scale in quarter notes. You can already play this without even thinking. Play through it watching the notation and say the name of each note to yourself as you play.

The next step is recognizing the notes in different octaves. Since the notes on the harmonica repeat in identical patterns over three octaves, you can easily play a scale by ear in any octave once you know it. Shown below is the notation for the **C** major scale played over two octaves in eighth notes and then sixteenth notes (see page 8). Don't let the notation for the higher notes scare you. They are simply repeats of the lower notes an octave higher. On the recording the harmonica has been omitted when the example repeats. Play along with the drum beat while reading the notation. Think the names of the notes as you go. Once you can do this with sixteenth notes, you are well on your way.

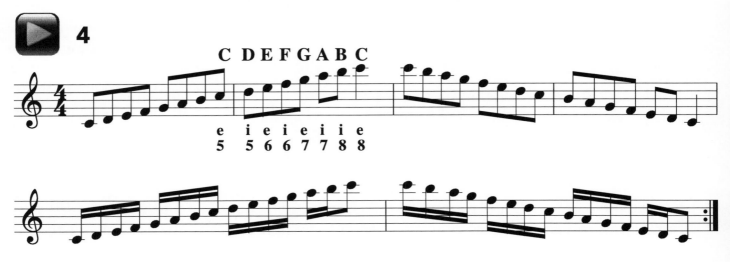

PLAYING SONGS

Once you have familiarized yourself with the notes on the chromatic harmonica by playing the C major scale, the best way to become comfortable with the instrument is to play songs. Over the next few pages you will learn some melodies which sound great on the chromatic harmonica. The first is the traditional Irish song **Londonderry Air**. All the notes come from the C major scale, and it covers a range of less than two octaves, so it is not difficult to play. Play it slowly and make sure you are producing a strong, even tone. Remember that you can listen to the recording to hear a demo of each song and copy it by ear if you have difficulty with the notation.

 5 Londonderry Air

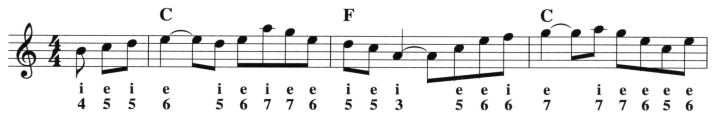

SLURS

A **slur** is a curved line above or below two or more different notes. It indicates that the notes must be played smoothly (called **legato**). To play legato, only tongue the **first** note of the group and keep blowing while you change your mouth position for the other notes.

 6 **Moreton Bay**

This Australian convict song has a mournful sound and should also be played slowly with a strong, even tone. It is written in ¾ time and covers a range of one and a half octaves. This song contains many slurs, which helps create a smooth, flowing sound. Slurs can be used any time for expression even when they are not indicated in the notation.

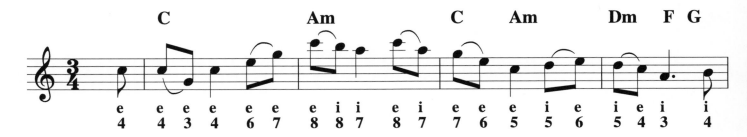

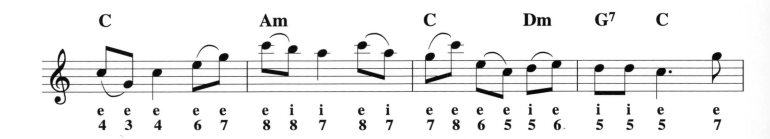

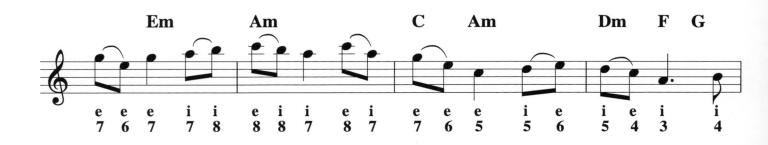

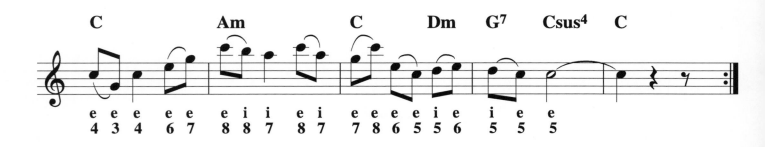

CUT COMMON TIME

The following song features a new time signature called **cut common time**, or simply cut time. It is indicated by the symbol ₵. Cut time is also called $\frac{2}{2}$ time and represents two half note beats per bar. In this situation, each half note receives one count. Whole notes receive two counts, while quarter notes receive half a count. Cut common time contains basic two beats per bar, but because eighth notes are used in cut common instead of sixteenth notes, it is easier to read.

To become a versatile harmonica player is worth learning to play all the melodies presented here on the diatonic harp as well as the chromatic. It is recommended that you learn as many songs as possible on both types of harp. Although the numbering is slightly different, almost everything else is the same if you are not using the slide. Players who are comfortable with both types of harmonica are highly sought after by other musicians.

7 Arkansas Traveller

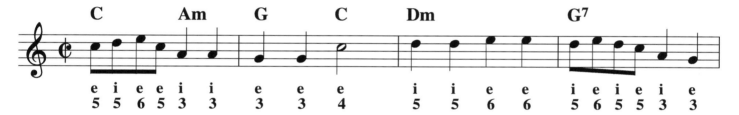

Here are two more melodies to help you become familiar with the layout of the chromatic harmonica. They both sound best when played at a fast tempo, but learn them slowly at first and then gradually increase the tempo once you are comfortable with the notes.

 8 The Irish Washerwoman

 9 When Johnny Comes Marching Home

This one is in a **minor key** (key of A minor). Minor keys are discussed in detail in lesson 10. Minor keys are generally said to have a sadder sound than major keys.

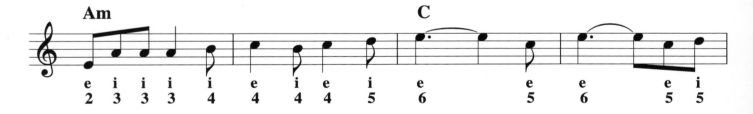

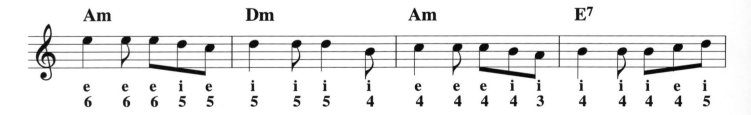

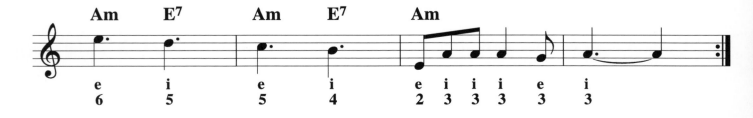

READING WITHOUT NUMBERS

By now you should be ready to play some songs without relying on the numbers and breath indicators. Once you can recognize the notes from the notation, the best way to develop your reading is by doing lots of it! The most enjoyable way to do this is to read melodies. Here are some to practice. Read each one until you can play it from memory and then close your eyes and concentrate on playing with feeling and a beautiful tone.

10 Brahms' Lullaby   J. Brahms

11 Shenandoah

The melodies presented here are only a few examples. It is recommended that you purchase a book of song melodies and start learning the ones in C major. By the end of this book, you will understand how to read melodies in all the other keys as well. It is also a good idea to work your way through method books for other wind instruments, particularly flute books, as the lowest note on the flute is **middle C** – the same as the lowest note on a **C** Chromatic harmonica.

12 The Happy Wanderer

LESSON TWO

SOLVING READING PROBLEMS

As you read through these melodies, notice how many different rhythms are used, but the notes remain the same. When you encounter problems in reading music, it is a good idea to practice pitch reading and rhythm reading separately, as most problems are one or the other and by separating them you can zero in on the exact thing you need to work on without any other complications.

Each time you solve a reading problem, you make it easier to solve the next one you encounter because many note sequences and rhythms occur again and again in music.

13 Into the Sun

P. Gelling

SWINGING NOTES

In styles such as Jazz, Blues and Gospel, eighth notes are often "swung". This means that the first eighth note in a group of two is twice as long as the first, having the time of the first two notes of an eighth note triplet. If the eighth notes in a piece of music are meant to be swung, you will often see the symbol ♫ = 𝄾 at the start of the piece.

The following example is another song in a minor key. Notice the mournful quality of the tonality. Read the notation and notice that the same notes are used as in C major, but the melody keeps returning to (and ends with) a **D** note rather than a C note. This is because it is in the key of D minor. Minor keys are discussed in more detail in lesson 10. For now, just notice that the sound is different when the same notes are used around a different central point.

 14   St James Infirmary

As indicated above, the eighth notes in this song are swung. If you are not familiar with swinging notes and have trouble with them, please refer to either *Progressive Beginner Harmonica* or *Progressive Beginner Blues Harmonica*.

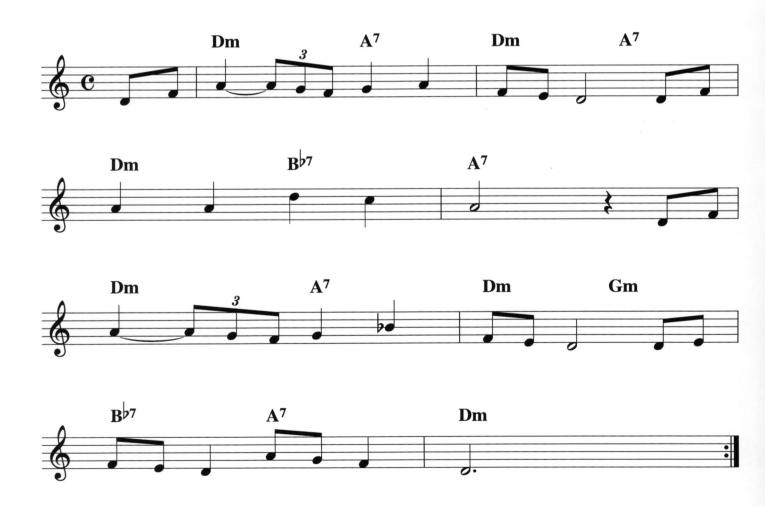

Here is another melody in the key of D minor using swung eighth notes.

15 Minor Swing (D minor)

P. Gelling

16 Minor Swing (A minor)

Here is the same melody in the key of A minor. Changing the key of a piece of music is called **transposing**. This is explained in lesson 7. On the recording, space has been left for you to play the melody along with the band.

RANGE OF THE CHROMATIC HARMONICA

It is possible to play over a range of three octaves on some chromatic harmonicas, while others cover four octaves. The three octave version is more common and is used for this book. If you have a four octave harmonica, it simply gives you an extra octave of all the notes. The distance of four octaves is shown on the keyboard below. The **lowest note** on the **C chromatic harmonica** is called **middle C**. On a **piano**, this is the C note in the **middle** of the keyboard as shown on the diagram below.

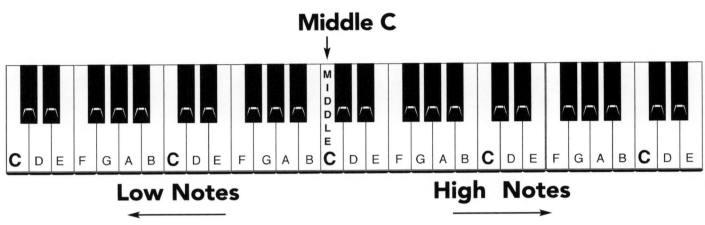

17 C Major Scale Over 3 Octaves

Here is the **C major scale** over **three octaves**. The third (high) octave has the symbol **8va** written above the music. This means it is played an octave higher than written. This symbol is often used for very high notes, as it makes them easier to read. When the notation returns to its normal pitch, the word **loco** is written above the music.

18 Scale Sequence

Playing the major scale on the chromatic harmonica is easy because you don't need to bend any note in any octave. However, the bigger body of the harmonica itself means that the size of the holes and the distance between them is different to that of the diatonic harmonica. Playing **sequences** is a good way of teaching your brain the distances.

SHARPS (♯) AND FLATS (♭)

Although there are only seven letter names used in music, there are actually **twelve** different notes used in music. The extra notes fall in between some of the letter names. These notes are indicated by the use of **sharps and flats**. A sharp is indicated by the symbol ♯ and means that the pitch is **raised by a semitone** (the smallest measurement used in western music). E.g. the note **C sharp (C♯)** is higher than C and falls halfway between the notes C and D. A flat is indicated by the symbol ♭ and means that the pitch is **lowered by a semitone**. E.g. the note **D♭** is lower than D and falls halfway between D and C. This means that the notes **C♯** and **D♭** are exactly the same. This may seem confusing but is easy to understand if you look at the piano keyboard shown in the diagram below. The white notes are all the natural notes (**A B C D E F G**) and the black notes are the sharps and flats. D♯ is the same as E♭, F♯ is the same as G♭, etc. Sometimes one is used and sometimes the other, depending on the musical situation and the **key** the music is written in. Keys are discussed further in lesson 6.

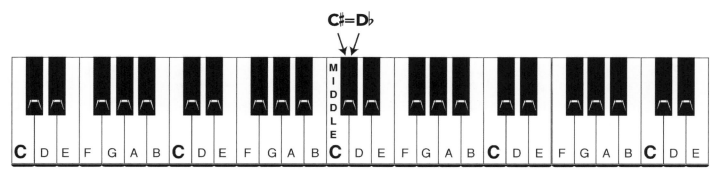

THE CHROMATIC SCALE

As mentioned above, with the inclusion of sharps and flats, there are **12** different notes within one octave. The notes **EF** and **BC** are always one **semitone** apart. All the other natural notes are a **tone** apart. Sharps (♯) and flats (♭) are found between the notes that are a tone apart. If you combine all the natural notes with the sharps and flats found in between them, you end up with what is called the **chromatic scale**. This scale contains all the notes used in music. The chromatic scale is made up of twelve consecutive semitones.

INTERVALS

An **interval** is the distance between any two notes. Intervals are named in numbers which are larger or smaller depending on how many letter names apart the notes are. E.g. C to D is the interval of a second (C=1, D=2), C to E is the interval of a third (C D E = 1 2 3), C to F is the interval of a fourth, etc. There are actually various different types of intervals (major, minor, etc). This is explained in detail in lesson 9. At this stage it is enough to be aware that different notes can be specific distances apart based on their letter names and the number of semitones between them, and that these distances are called intervals. If you wish to pursue music more seriously, it is important to understand and be able to hear all the different intervals. Any good keyboard or theory teacher will be able to help you with this.

USING THE SLIDE

As you learnt in lesson 1, there are **two rows of holes** on the chromatic harmonica. The **top** row contains **all the natural notes**. The bottom row is blocked unless you press in the slide. When you depress the slide, it opens the bottom row which contains all the sharps and flats and at the same time blocks off the top row of notes. The use of the slide gives you **24** holes instead of 12. This is demonstrated in the diagrams below.

TOP ROW OF NOTES

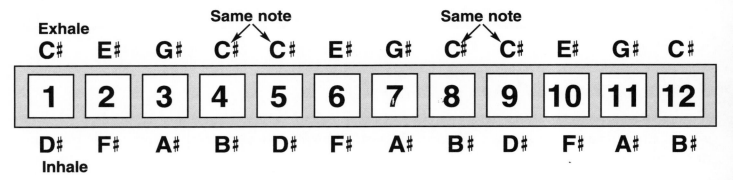

Same note   Same note

Exhale
C E G C C E G C C E G C

| 1 | 2 | 3 | 4 | 5 | 6 | 7 | 8 | 9 | 10 | 11 | 12 |

D F A B D F A B D F A B

Inhale

BOTTOM ROW OF NOTES (Activated by the Slide)

The bottom row of notes are all shown as sharps here. Each one could be described another way by using flat or natural signs. These are **enharmonic notes** and are explained on page 27.

Same note   Same note

Exhale
C♯ E♯ G♯ C♯ C♯ E♯ G♯ C♯ C♯ E♯ G♯ C♯

| 1 | 2 | 3 | 4 | 5 | 6 | 7 | 8 | 9 | 10 | 11 | 12 |

D♯ F♯ A♯ B♯ D♯ F♯ A♯ B♯ D♯ F♯ A♯ B♯

Inhale

 19 Using the Slide to Play Sharps

All sharps and flats are played on the chromatic harp by using the slide. When the slide is pushed in, both inhale and exhale notes sound **one semitone higher** than they do without the slide pushed in, thus creating a **sharpened** version of the natural note. In the following example, each time the slide is pushed in, the note has an **S** below it. Follow the notation while listening to the recording and then try playing it. It is important to release the slide as you begin to play the next note. Don't worry if you have trouble with this, the example is simply a demonstration to show you how it works. With practice it gets easier and easier.

Sometimes a sharp or flat occurs only once in a piece. In this traditional British folk song, the note **F#** occurs only in bar 15 . This note is played by inhaling through hole **6** and pushing in the slide. Release the slide just as you begin to breathe out to play the following **G** note.

 20 The Ash Grove

MORE ABOUT MAJOR SCALES

As you learnt in lesson 1, the **C major scale** contains the following notes.

C   D   E F   G   A   B C

tone	tone	semitone	tone	tone	tone	semitone
T	**T**	**ST**	**T**	**T**	**T**	**ST**

The distance between each note is a tone except for **EF** and **BC** where the distance is only a semitone. A **semitone** is the smallest distance between two notes used in western music. Shown below is the pattern of tones and semitones in the major scale, with the **scale degrees** written under the notes.

Note	C	D	E	F	G	A	B	C
Scale Degree	1	2	3	4	5	6	7	8
Tone Pattern		T	T	ST	T	T	T	ST

T = Tone
ST = Semitone

MAJOR SCALE PATTERN

Once you know the pattern of tones and semitones used to create the C major scale, you can build a major scale on **any** of the twelve notes used in music. It is important to memorize this pattern, which is shown below.

Tone   Tone   Semitone   Tone   Tone   Tone   Semitone

The **semitones** are always found between the **3rd and 4th**, and **7th and 8th** degrees of the scale. All the other notes are a tone apart.

THE G MAJOR SCALE

To demonstrate how the major scale pattern works starting on any note, here is the **G major scale**. Notice that the 7th degree is F sharp (**F#**) instead of F. This is done to maintain the correct pattern of tones and semitones and thus retain the sound of the major scale (**do re mi fa so la ti do**).

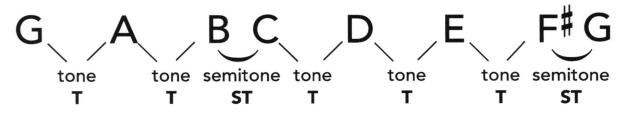

G   A   B C   D   E   F# G

tone	tone	semitone	tone	tone	tone	semitone
T	**T**	**ST**	**T**	**T**	**T**	**ST**

Here is the notation for the G major scale. The F♯ note is the same as the one you learnt to play earlier in **The Ash Grove** (hole 6 inhaled with the slide pushed in).

 21 G Major Scale

KEY SIGNATURES

When a song consists of notes from a particular scale, it is said to be written in the **key** which has the same name as that scale. For example, if a song contains notes from the **G major scale**, it is said to be in the **key of G major**. Instead of writing a sharp sign before every **F♯** note, it is easier to write just one sharp sign after the treble clef. This means that **all** F notes on the staff are played as F♯, even though there is no sharp sign placed before the note. This is called a **Key Signature**. Key signatures are discussed in more detail in lesson 6.

 22   Brahms' Lullaby in the key of G

Play all F notes as **F♯** as indicated by the key signature.

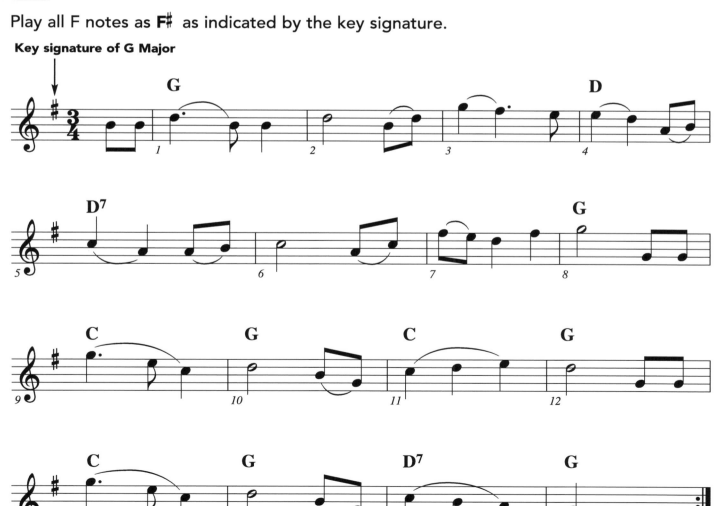

THE F MAJOR SCALE

By starting the major scale pattern on the note F, it is possible to create an **F major scale**. In this scale, it is necessary to flatten the 4th degree from B to **B♭** to maintain the correct pattern of tones and semitones.

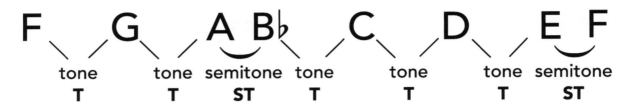

 23 F Major Scale

Here is the F major scale written in standard notation with the scale degrees written under the notes. The B flat note is played by **inhaling** through the **3rd** hole and pressing in the slide.

 24 All Through the Night

This melody is derived from the F major scale and is therefore said to be in the **key of F major**. Play all B notes as **B♭** as indicated by the key signature.

Key signature of F Major

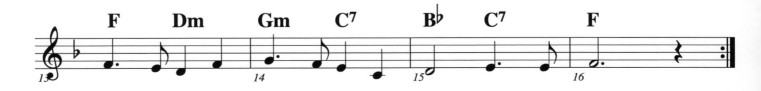

LESSON FIVE

PLAYING THE CHROMATIC SCALE

In the previous examples, the melody consisted entirely of notes from the major scale. However, many melodies use notes from outside the major scale, particularly in styles such as Blues, Jazz, Rock and Funk. These "outside notes" relate to the chromatic scale starting on the same note as the major scale of the key the music is written in. Therefore, if you have a piece of music in the key of C which contains notes which are not in the C major scale, you can relate these notes to the **C chromatic scale**.

 25 C Chromatic Scale

This example demonstrates one octave of the C chromatic scale. The notes played with the slide depressed have an **S** under them, with the correct hole number written underneath.

ENHARMONIC NOTES

The "in between" notes in the chromatic scale can be described as either sharps or flats. These are called **enharmonic** notes, which means they are the same pitch (e.g C♯ =D♭ and F♯ =G♭). Here is an example demonstrating the use of enharmonic notes.

 26 Song of the Camel

P. Gelling

You now know all the different notes used in western music (twelve in all). This includes all the natural notes (**A B C D E F G**), plus **F#**, **C#**, **G#**, **D#**, and **A#**. Because each sharp note has another name as a flat, you also know **G♭**, **D♭**, **A♭**, **E♭**, and **B♭**. If you play all twelve notes in succession, you get the **chromatic scale**. As you know, all of the notes in a chromatic scale are **one semitone** apart. To get to know all possible ways of describing any note in a given key, it is a good idea to call all notes which are not natural to the key **sharps when ascending** and **flats when descending**.

Like all scales, you will need to be able to play the chromatic scale across the whole range of the harmonica. The following example demonstrates two octaves of the **C chromatic scale**. Take it slowly at first until you can play it smoothly and easily without hesitation. It is a good idea to make the chromatic scale part of your daily practice, as a good knowledge of this scale makes it easy to quickly transpose any melody, as well as making it easier to learn any new scale or key.

27 C Chromatic Scale Over 2 Octaves

Once you can play the C chromatic scale, you already know all other chromatic scales, e.g. to play the **E chromatic scale**, you simply start on the note **E** and play all possible notes until you arrive at the next E note one octave higher or lower. This is demonstrated in the following example which contains two octaves of the E chromatic scale.

28 E Chromatic Scale Over 2 Octaves

THE NATURAL SIGN

 This is a **natural** sign.

29

A natural sign cancels the effect of a sharp or flat for the rest of that bar, or until another sharp or flat sign occurs within that bar. Notice the alteration between **G** natural (**G♮**) and **G♯** in example 29.

THE BLUES SCALE

An essential scale for all harmonica players to know is the **blues scale**. Its degrees are **1 ♭3 4 ♭5 ♮5** and **♭7**. In the key of **C** the notes would be **C E♭ F G♭ G♮** and **B♭**. In the key of **D** the notes would be **D F G A♭ A♮** and **C**, etc. For a basic introduction to the Blues scale, see *Progressive Beginner Harmonica* or *Progressive Beginner Blues Harmonica*. The following 12 bar Blues solo is derived from the **D** Blues scale and makes use of **sharp**, **flat** and **natural** signs. The only note requiring the use of the slide is **G♯** or **A♭**, which is an **exhale** note on the **3rd** hole with the slide depressed.

30 Slow and Easy

P. Gelling

MORE ABOUT KEYS AND KEY SIGNATURES

The **key** describes the note around which a piece of music is built. When a song consists of notes from a particular scale, it is said to be written in the **key** which has the same notes as that scale. For example, if a song contains mostly notes from the **C major scale**, it is said to be in the **key of C major**. If a song contains mostly notes from the **F major scale**, it is said to be in the **key of F major**. If a song contains mostly notes from the **G major scale**, it is said to be in the **key of G major**. When playing in any major key other than C, the key will contain at least one sharp or flat, and possibly as many as six. Instead of writing these sharps or flats before each note as they occur, they are usually written at the beginning of the song just before the time signature. These sharps or flats are called a **key signature**. The number of sharps or flats in the key signature depends on the number of sharps or flats in the corresponding major scale. The major scales and key signatures for the keys of **G** and **F** are shown below. Without sharps and flats, these scales would not contain the correct pattern of tones and semitones and would therefore not sound like a major scale.

G Major Scale

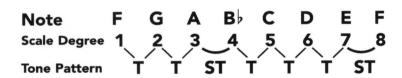

Note	G	A	B	C	D	E	F♯	G
Scale Degree	1	2	3	4	5	6	7	8
Tone Pattern		T	T	ST	T	T	T	ST

Key Signature of G Major

The **G major** scale contains one sharp, F♯, therefore the key signature for the key of **G major** contains one sharp, F♯.

F Major Scale

Note	F	G	A	B♭	C	D	E	F
Scale Degree	1	2	3	4	5	6	7	8
Tone Pattern		T	T	ST	T	T	T	ST

Key Signature of F Major

The **F major** scale contains one flat, B♭, therefore the key signature for the key of **F major** contains one flat, B♭.

The reason some scales contain sharps while others contain flats is that there has to be a separate letter name for each note in the scale. E.g. the G major scale contains F♯ instead of G♭ even though these two notes are identical in sound. However, if G♭ was used, the scale would contain two notes with the letter name G and no note with the letter name F. This is the reason for choosing to call the note F♯ in this key. In the key of F major, the note B♭ is chosen instead of A♯ for the same reason. If A♯ was used, the scale would contain two notes with the letter name A and no note with the letter name B. The note each major scale starts on will determine how many sharps or flats are found in each key signature because of the necessity for the scale to have the correct pattern of tones and semitones in order to sound right. The charts on the following page contain the key signatures of all the major scales used in music, along with the number of sharps or flats contained in each key. Because there are 12 notes used in music, this means there are 12 possible starting notes for major scales (including sharps and flats). This means that some of the keys will have sharps or flats in their name, e.g. F♯ major, B♭ major, E♭ major, etc. Keys which contain sharps are called sharp keys and keys which contain flats are called flat keys.

SHARP KEY SIGNATURES

	G Major	D Major	A Major	E Major	B Major	F# Major
Sharps	F#	F#C#	F#C#G#	F#C#G#D#	F#C#G#D#A#	F#C#G#D#A#E#

*The new sharp **key** is a fifth interval * higher*

Key	Number of Sharps	Sharp Notes
G	1	F#
D	2	F#, C#
A	3	F#, C#, G#
E	4	F#, C#, G#, D#
B	5	F#, C#, G#, D#, A#,
F#	6	F#, C#, G#, D#, A#, E#

*The new sharp **note** is a fifth interval * higher*

FLAT KEY SIGNATURES

	F Major	B♭ Major	E♭ Major	A♭ Major	D♭ Major	G♭ Major
Flats	B♭	B♭E♭	B♭E♭A♭	B♭E♭A♭D♭	B♭E♭A♭D♭G♭	B♭E♭A♭D♭G♭C♭

*The new flat **key** is a fourth interval * higher*

Key	Number of Flats	Flat Notes
F	1	B♭
B♭	2	B♭, E♭
E♭	3	B♭, E♭, A♭
A♭	4	B♭, E♭, A♭, D♭
D♭	5	B♭, E♭, A♭, D♭, G♭,
G♭	6	B♭, E♭, A♭, D♭, G♭, C♭

*The new flat **note** is a fourth interval * higher*

* Intervals are dealt with in detail in lesson 9.

LESSON SEVEN

TRANSPOSING

Transposing (or transposition) means changing the key of a piece of music. This can apply to a scale, a phrase, a short melody, or an entire song. The ability to transpose is an essential skill for all musicians to develop. The easiest way to transpose is to write the **scale degrees** under the original melody and then work out which notes correspond to those scale degrees in the key you want to transpose to. You should work towards being able to do this in your head instantly, without the need for notated scale degrees. Written below is a short melody played in the key of **C** and then transposed to the keys of **F** and **G**. Play through them and notice that the melody sounds the same, but the overall pitch may be higher or lower. Transpose this melody to all other major keys. You should also try this same technique with other tunes you know. The more you do this, the easier it gets, and the better you are at transposing, the easier it will be to play Jazz.

 31   Melody in C

Scale Degrees: 1 6 5 3 2 4 5 6 7 1

 32   Same Melody in F

Scale Degrees: 1 6 5 3 2 4 5 6 7 1

 33   Same Melody in G

Scale Degrees: 1 6 5 3 2 4 5 6 7 1

THE KEY CYCLE

There are many reasons why you need to be able to play equally well in every key. Bands often have to play in keys that suit their singer. That could be **F#** or **Db** for example. Keyboard players tend to like the keys of **C**, **F** and **G**, while **E** and **A** are fairly common keys for guitar. Horn players like flat keys such as **F**, **Bb** and **Eb**. Apart from this, Jazz tunes often contain many key changes in themselves. For these reasons, you need to learn how keys relate to each other so you can move quickly between them.

One way to do this is to use the **key cycle** (also called the **cycle of 5ths** or **cycle of 4ths**). It contains the names of all the keys and is fairly easy to memorize.

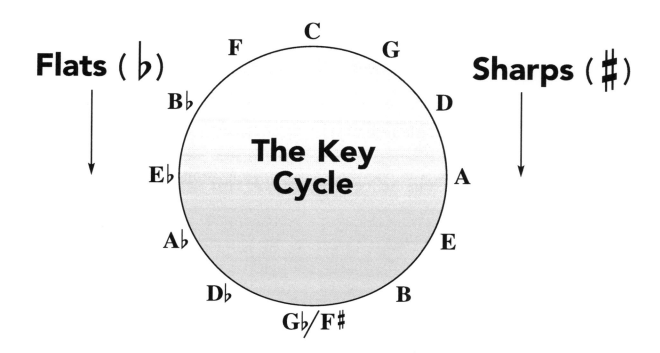

Think of the key cycle like a clock. Just as there are 12 points on the clock, there are also 12 keys. **C** is at the top and contains no sharps or flats. Moving around clockwise you will find the next key is **G**, which contains one sharp (**F#**). The next key is **D**, which contains two sharps (**F#** and **C#**). Progressing further through the sharp keys each key contains an extra sharp, with the new sharp being the 7th note of the new key, and the others being any which were contained in the previous key. Therefore the key of A would automatically contain F# and C# which were in the key of D, plus G# which is the 7th note of the A major scale. When you get to F# (at 6 o'clock), the new sharp is called E# which is enharmonically the same as **F**. Remember that **enharmonic** means two different ways of writing the same note. Another example of enharmonic spelling would be **F#** and **Gb**. This means that **Gb** could become the name of the key of **F#**. The key of **F#** contains six sharps, while the key of **Gb** contains six flats – all of which are exactly the same notes.

If you start at **C** again at the top of the cycle and go anticlockwise you will progress through the flat keys. The key of **F** contains one flat (**Bb**), which then becomes the name of the next key around the cycle. In flat keys, the new flat is always the 4th degree of the new key. Continuing around the cycle, the key of **Bb** contains two flats (**Bb** and **Eb**) and so on. **Practice playing all the notes around the cycle both clockwise and anticlockwise**. Once you can do this, play a **major scale** starting on each note of the cycle. In Jazz, there is a lot of movement around the cycle, so the more familiar you are with it, the better.

MAJOR SCALES IN ALL KEYS

The following example demonstrates one octave of the major scale ascending and descending in every key. This will take some time to learn but is essential for anyone wanting to play Jazz or Classical music. Learning scales may not seem as interesting as playing melodies, but a little effort at this stage will pay off very well later on, regardless of the style of music you are playing. Memorize the notes of each scale and then try playing it with your eyes closed while visualizing how the notation for the scale would look. Once you have learnt all the scales, you will be able to read music better, play melodies confidently in any key and be able to improvise in any key much more easily.

34

USING THE KEY CYCLE

A good way to become more confident playing in all keys is to take a phrase and play it in every key in order of sharps and flats around the key cycle as shown in the following example which moves around the cycle anticlockwise (adding a new flat for each new key and then continuing through the sharp keys). It is also important to repeat the process going clockwise around the cycle. Write the scale degrees under the notes at first if necessary, and sing them to yourself as you play. If you hope to play Jazz, this ability is essential, as the majority of Jazz tunes modulate around the key cycle in this manner. Make this process part of your everyday practice. The eventual aim is to be able to pick up your instrument and be able to play any melody in any key instantly.

35 Major Scale Phrase in all Keys

LESSON EIGHT

MORE ABOUT BLUES SCALES

Like the major scale, it is important to be comfortable with the Blues scale in every key. The following example demonstrates the Blues scale moving **around the cycle** through all the keys. Once again, memorize each one and then connect them together until you can play the whole example smoothly and evenly without looking at the notation. Then try reversing the order of the keys.

 36 Blues Scales in all Keys

Once you are comfortable with the scales themselves, try inventing a short riff from the Blues scale in one key and then playing the riff in all keys as shown in the following example. If you have trouble with this, memorise all the scale degrees of the riff before transposing it. The riff shown here begins on the flattened 7th degree of the key.

 37 Blues Scale Phrase in all Keys

PLAYING OCTAVES

Playing octaves on the chromatic can be difficult at first because the notes are four holes apart. This means you have to block the holes in between with your tongue. The following example is a demonstration of several pairs of octaves on the chromatic harmonica. Practice the technique using exhale and inhale notes in one position before trying the whole exercise. It is difficult so be patient and practice it for a short time each day among your other exercises. Once you can do the basic exercise, try playing some scales in octaves as demonstrated in example 39.

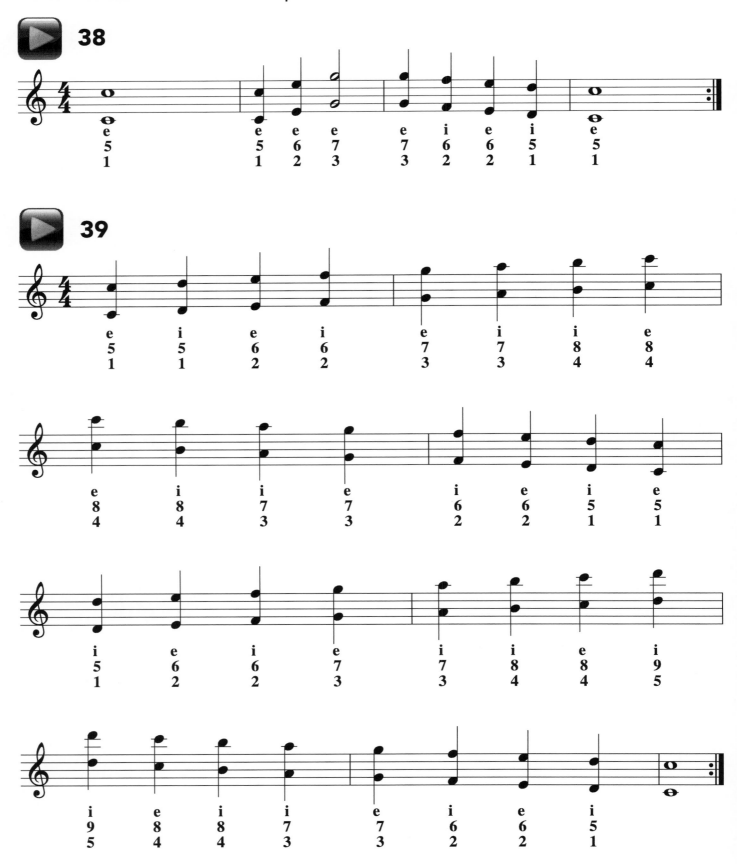

The next step is to play some melodies in octaves as shown here. There are no breathing indications under the notes here, but you already know all the notes so this shouldn't be a problem. If you have trouble, simply listen to the recording and imitate the sounds you hear.

 40 When the Saints go Marching in

 41 Lonely Hours

P. Gelling

This one is a Blues in the key of D minor. To hear great examples of playing octaves on the chromatic harp, listen to Blues players like Little Walter, James Cotton and George "Harmonica" Smith. Be patient with this technique as it takes quite some time to master.

THE KEY OF E♭ MINOR

By keeping the slide **permanently depressed**, it is possible to play third position in the key of **E♭ minor** in a similar manner to the keys of A minor or **D** minor. You can test this by pressing in the slide and playing any melody you already know in D minor (e.g. St James Infirmary or Minor Swing). To play the **E** Blues scale, you only need to release the slide for one note (**A** natural – the flattened fifth degree). The following example demonstrates two octaves of the **E♭** Blues scale.

42   Blues Scale in E Flat

43   Falling Down Blues

P. Gelling

Here is a Blues solo derived from the **E♭** Blues scale. Notice the use of octaves here.

UNDERSTANDING INTERVALS

An interval is the distance between two musical notes. Intervals are measured in numbers, and are calculated by counting the number of letter names (**A B C D E F G A**) between and including the notes being measured. Within an octave, intervals are: **Unison** (two notes of the same pitch played or sung together or consecutively), **2nd**, **3rd**, **4th**, **5th**, **6th**, **7th** and **Octave** (two notes an octave apart). Thus **A** to **B** is a **2nd** interval, as is B to C, C to D etc. **A** to **C** is a **3rd** interval, **A** to **D** is a **4th**, **A** to **E** is a **5th**, **A** to **F** is a **6th**, **A** to **G** is a **7th** and **A** to the next **A** is an **octave**.

Intervals may be **melodic** (two notes played consecutively) or **harmonic** (two notes played at the same time). Hence two people singing at the same time are said to be singing in harmony.

INTERVAL QUALITIES

Different intervals have different qualities, as shown below:

Quality	Can be applied to
Perfect	Unisons, 4ths, 5ths and Octaves
Major	2nds, 3rds, 6ths and 7ths
Minor	2nds, 3rds, 6ths and 7ths
Augmented	All intervals
Diminished	All intervals

These intervals can be best explained with the aid of a chromatic scale. If you look at the one below, it is easy to see that since intervals are measured in semitones, they may begin or end on a sharp or flat rather than a natural note.

$$A \quad \frac{A\#}{B\flat} \quad B \quad C \quad \frac{C\#}{D\flat} \quad D \quad \frac{D\#}{E\flat} \quad E \quad F \quad \frac{F\#}{G\flat} \quad G \quad \frac{G\#}{A\flat} \quad A$$

Perfect intervals are **4ths**, **5ths** and **octaves**. If you **widen** a perfect interval by a semitone it becomes **augmented** (added to). E.g. if you add a semitone to the perfect 4th interval **C** to **F**, it becomes the **augmented 4th interval C** to **F♯**. Notice that the letter name remains the same – it is not referred to as C to G♭.

If you narrow a perfect interval by a semitone they become **diminished** (lessened). E.g. if you lessen the perfect 5th interval **D** to **A** by a semitone, it becomes the **diminished 5th interval D to A♭**. Again, the letter name remains the same – it is not referred to as D to G♯.

Major intervals (2nds, 3rds, 6ths and 7ths) become minor if narrowed by a semitone and **minor** intervals become major if widened by a semitone. A **diminished** interval can be created by narrowing a perfect or minor interval by a semitone. An **augmented** interval can be created by widening a perfect or major interval by a semitone.

INTERVAL DISTANCES

In summary, here is a list of the distances of all common intervals up to an octave measured in semitones. Each new interval is one semitone wider apart than the previous one. Notice that the interval of an octave is exactly twelve semitones. This is because there are twelve different notes in the chromatic scale. Notice also that the interval which has a distance of six semitones can be called either an augmented 4th or a diminished 5th. This interval is also often called a **tritone** (6 semitones = 3 tones).

Minor 2nd – One semitone

Major 2nd – Two semitones

Minor 3rd – Three semitones

Major 3rd – Four semitones

Perfect 4th – Five semitones

Augmented 4th or Diminished 5th – Six semitones

Perfect 5th – Seven semitones

Minor 6th – Eight semitones

Major 6th – Nine semitones

Minor 7th – Ten semitones

Major 7th – Eleven semitones

Perfect Octave – Twelve semitones

The following example demonstrates all of the common intervals ascending within one octave starting and ending on the note C.

44 All Intervals up to an Octave

minor 2nd   major 2nd   minor 3rd   major 3rd

perfect 4th   diminished 5th   perfect 5th   minor 6th

major 6th   minor 7th   major 7th   perfect octave

IDENTIFYING INTERVALS BY EAR

Since **all melodies are made up of a series of intervals**, it is essential to learn to identify intervals by ear and be able to reproduce them at will both with your voice and on your instrument. If you can sing something accurately, it means you are hearing it accurately. Here are some ways of developing your ability to identify and reproduce intervals. The example given in the first two exercises is a minor 3rd, but it is essential to go through these processes with **all** intervals.

1.   Choose an interval you wish to work on (e.g. minor 3rds). Play a starting note (e.g. C) and sing it. Then sing a minor 3rd up from that note (E♭). Hold the note in your mind while you test its accuracy on your instrument. Then choose another starting note and repeat the process. Keep doing this until you are accurate every time. The next step is to sing the interval (in this case a minor 3rd) downwards from your starting note. Again, do this repeatedly until you are accurate every time.

2.   Sing the same interval consecutively upwards and then downwards several times. E.g. start on C and sing a minor 3rd up from it (E♭). Then sing a minor 3rd up from E♭ (G♭). Then another minor third up from G♭ (B♭♭ – which is enharmonically the same as A). Then up another minor 3rd (C an octave higher than the starting note). Once you can do this, reverse the process (start on C and sing a minor 3rd down to A, then another minor 3rd down and then another, etc).

3.   Play and sing a starting note (e.g. C) and then think of it as the first degree of the chromatic scale – sing "one". Now sing the flattened second degree of the scale – sing "flat two". This note is a minor 2nd up from your C note (a D♭ note). Then sing the C again ("one"). Then sing the second degree of the scale (a D note – sing "two"). Next, sing your C note again ("one"). Continue in this manner all the way up the chromatic scale until you reach C an octave above. The entire sequence goes: 1, ♭2, 1, 2, 1, ♭3, 1, 3, 1, 4, 1, ♭5, 1, 5, 1, ♭6, 1, 6, 1, ♭7, 1, 7, 1, 8, 1. As with the previous exercises, once you can do this accurately (check your pitches on your instrument), reverse the process and sing downwards from the top of the scale, working your way down the chromatic scale again. The downward sequence goes 1(8), 7, 1, ♭7, 1, 6, 1, ♭6, 1, 5, 1, ♭5, 1, 4, 1, 3, 1, ♭3, 1, 2, 1, ♭2, 1, 1, 1(8).

4.   As well as hearing intervals melodically (one note at a time), it is important to be able to hear them harmonically (two notes played together). A good way to develop this is to have a friend play random harmonic intervals on either guitar or keyboard while you identify them. Keep your back to the instrument while you do this, so that you cannot identify the intervals by sight.

It is important to work at these things regularly until they become easy. Don't get frustrated if you can't hear intervals accurately at first. Most people have trouble with this. If you work at it for several months, you will see a dramatic improvement in your musical hearing, and will be able to improvise much more freely as well as being able to work out parts from recordings more easily.

Here are some exercises to help you become more comfortable playing in any key. Each one is written in a different key, but they are intended to be played in all keys. The first one is a sequence in the key of **D major**.

45

46

This one alternates between the note **B** and every other note in the **B major scale**, both ascending and descending.

47

Don't forget to practice the **chromatic scale** in every key. Here it is in the key of **G♭**.

48

Finally, here is one which alternates between the note **A** and every other note in the **A chromatic scale**, once again ascending and descending.

The following example demonstrates a melody in the key of **C** which contains notes from outside the major scale.

 49 Key of C

The following examples demonstrate the same melody transposed to the keys of **F** and **G**. Once again, you should transpose it to all the other keys. Before doing this it is worth learning to play the chromatic scale starting on any note. If you do this, it will be easier to play melodies in any key and also make it easier to transpose any melody that you learn in any key.

 50 Key of F

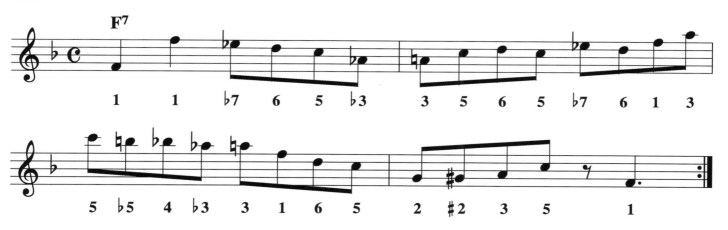

 51 Key of G

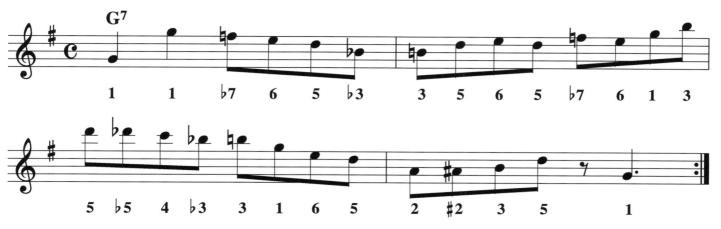

Here is a **Jazz Blues** solo in the key of **F** which makes use of many different intervals. Go through it and analyze the intervals and also the scale degrees against the **F chromatic scale**. Notice the use of both major and minor 3rd degrees, as well as the flattened 5th and 7th degrees of the scale. The ♭**3**, ♭**5** and ♭**7** are known as **blue notes** and are particularly common in all forms of Blues. As with many previous examples, the harmonica has been omitted from the recording on the repeat to leave space for you to play the solo with the band. You should also try improvising with the backing.

52 Blue Note Blues

P. Gelling

Here is a famous Ragtime melody written by **Scott Joplin**. Originally written for piano, it also sounds great on chromatic harmonica. It is well worth looking for other pieces originally written for other instruments and learning to play them on the chromatic.

53 The Entertainer

S. Joplin

LESSON TEN

MINOR KEYS AND SCALES

Apart from major keys, the other basic tonality used in traditional western music is a **minor key**. Songs in a minor key use notes taken from a minor scale. There are three basic types of minor scale — the **natural minor scale**, the **harmonic minor scale** and the **melodic minor scale**. Written below is the **A natural minor** scale. The degrees of the scale as they would relate to the major scale are written under the note names.

 54   A Natural Minor

The A natural minor contains exactly the same notes as the C major scale. The difference is that it starts and finishes on an **A** note instead of a C note. The A note then becomes the key note. Memorize both the scale degrees and the pattern of tones and semitones which make up the scale, then play it with your eyes closed, mentally naming the degrees as you play.

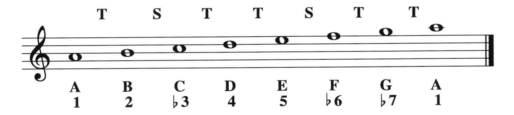

 55   The Gypsy's Tale   **P. Gelling**

Here is a melody in the **key of A minor** which is derived from the **A natural minor scale**. Learn it and then try making up your own melodies based on the ideas presented here.

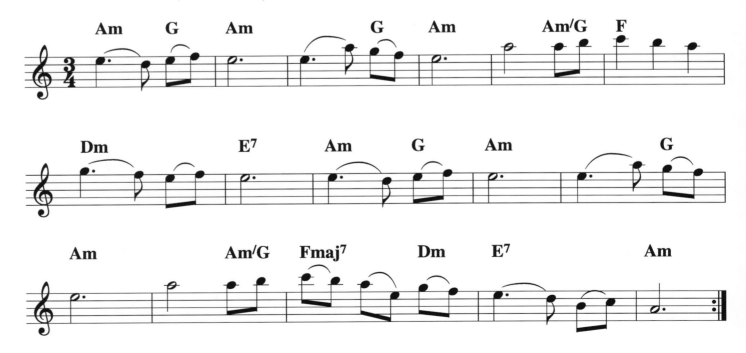

THE HARMONIC MINOR SCALE

The harmonic minor scale has a distance of 1½ tones between the **6th** and **7th** degrees. The raised 7th degree is the only difference between the harmonic minor and the natural minor. This scale is often described as having an "Eastern" sound.

 56 A Harmonic Minor

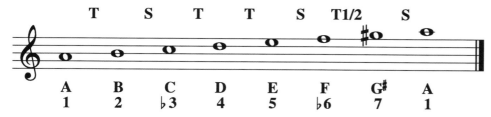

 57 Hahvah Nageelah

This famous melody is derived from the notes of the harmonic minor scale. It also features the **fermata** or pause sign ⌢ , which is used to indicate that a note or chord is held at the player's own discretion.

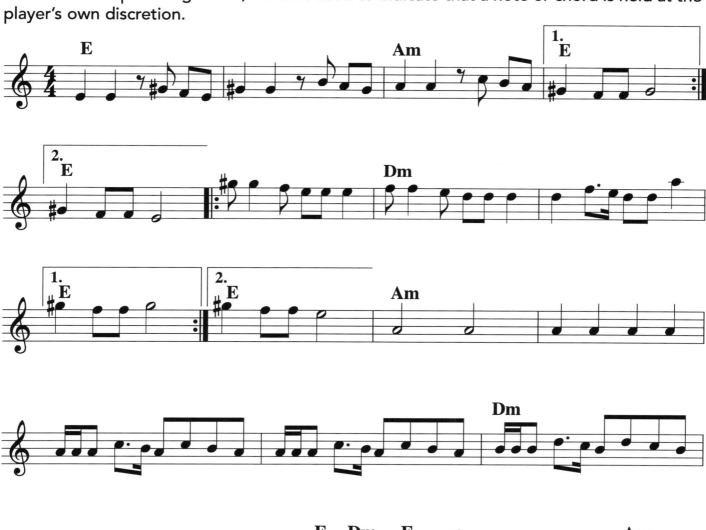

THE MELODIC MINOR SCALE

In the **A melodic minor** scale the **6th** and **7th** notes are sharpened when ascending and returned to natural when descending. This is the way the melodic minor is used in Classical music. However, in Jazz and other more modern styles, the melodic minor descends the same way it ascends. An easy way to think of the ascending melodic minor is as a major scale with a flattened third degree.

 58 A Melodic Minor

Melodies in minor keys often contain notes from more than one type of minor scale. The song Greensleeves is mostly derived from the melodic minor, but also contains a flattened 7th degree which comes from the natural minor.

 59 Greensleeves

LESSON ELEVEN

RELATIVE KEYS

If you compare the **A natural minor** scale with the **C major** scale you will notice that they contain the same notes (but start on a different note). Because of this, these two scales are referred to as "relatives"; **A minor** is the relative minor of **C major** and vice versa.

Major Scale: C Major

Relative Minor Scale: A Natural Minor

The harmonic and melodic minor scale variations are also relatives of the same major scale, e.g. **A harmonic** and **A melodic minor** are relatives of **C major**.

For every major scale (and every major chord) there is a relative minor scale which is based upon the **6th note** of the major scale. This is outlined in the table below.

MAJOR KEY (I)	C	D♭	D	E♭	E	F	F♯	G♭	G	A♭	A	B♭	B
RELATIVE MINOR KEY (VI)	Am	B♭m	Bm	Cm	C♯m	Dm	D♯m	E♭m	Em	Fm	F♯m	Gm	G♯m

Both the major and the relative minor share the same key signature, as illustrated below.

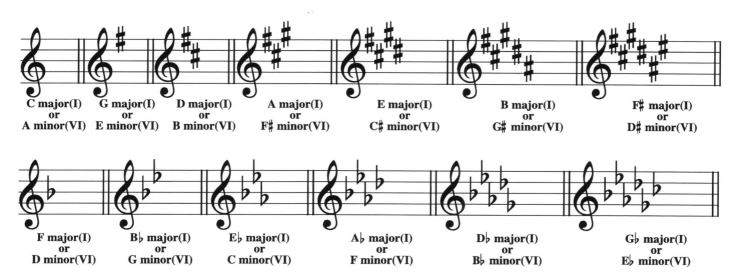

To determine whether a song is in a major key or the relative minor key, look at the last note or chord of the song. Songs often finish on the root note or the root chord. E.g., if the key signature contained one sharp, and the last chord of the song was **Em**, the key would probably be **E minor**, not **G major**. Minor key signatures are always based on the natural minor scale. The sharpened 6th and 7th degrees from the harmonic and melodic minor scales are not indicated in the key signature. This usually means there are accidentals (temporary sharps, flats or naturals) in melodies created from these scales.

Here is a popular South American folk song which moves between the keys of **A minor** and **C major** which are relative keys. This melody makes use of both the harmonic minor and the natural minor. Notice the *rit* symbol at the end indicating a gradual slowing down of the tempo.

When playing traditional melodies, many young players think "oh this is easy and boring, I'd rather be improvising". However, a simple melody played expressively with conviction and a good tone can move people a lot more than a fast nonsensical solo. It is easy to cover up musical inadequacies with a lot of fast notes. Listen carefully to the sound you are making as you play the melody and notice any weaknesses in tone, intonation, expression or rhythm which you may need to work on.

 60 El Condor Pasa

Here is a piece which alternates between the key of **D minor** and its relative – **F major**. Both these keys share the same key signature which contains one flat (**B♭**). The **C♯** note which occurs in this melody comes from the **D harmonic minor** scale. The piece is written in a **Baroque** style. The most famous composer from this period is **Johann Sebastian Bach**, who was a master at writing both melodically and harmonically at the same time. The harmonica did not exist in Bach's time, but one of his famous flute pieces "Siciliano" can be found on page 57.

 ## 61   Perpetual Motion

P. Gelling

The accompaniment on the recording of this piece is played on a harpsichord. The whole melody is played by the harmonica and then the accompaniment repeats so you can provide the melody. This piece may take some time to master but is well worth learning.

LEARNING A NEW MINOR KEY

The process for learning a new minor key is the same as that of a major key, except that there is more than one scale involved. You will need to know the notes of the natural, harmonic and melodic minor both theoretically and on the harmonica. Written below are the notes of these three scales in the key of **C minor. Remember that the descending melodic minor is identical to the natural minor.** Learn these scales from memory and then play the following example.

C Natural minor = C D E♭ F G A♭ B♭
Formula – 1 2 ♭3 4 5 ♭6 ♭7

C Harmonic minor = C D E♭ F G A♭ B
Formula – 1 2 ♭3 4 5 ♭6 7

C Melodic minor = C D E♭ F G A B (ascending)
Formula – 1 2 ♭3 4 5 6 7

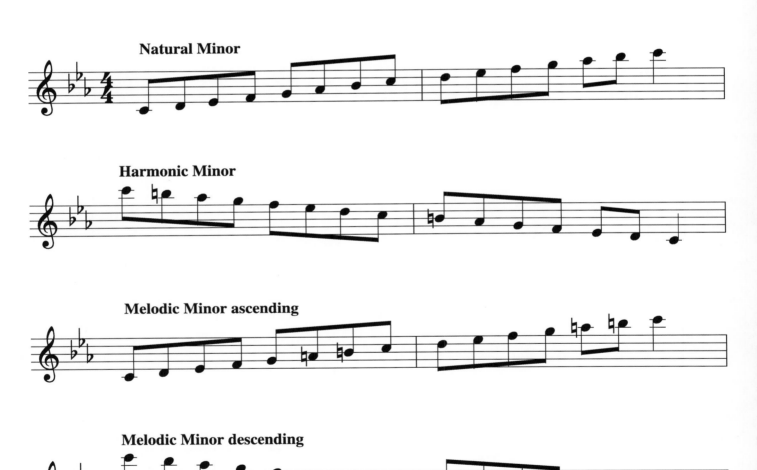

Natural Minor

Harmonic Minor

Melodic Minor ascending

Melodic Minor descending

MINOR SCALES IN ALL KEYS

By simply following the formula for each type of minor scale, either by scale degrees or pattern of tones and semitones, it is possible to create any of the minor scales from any starting note. E.g. if you know that the **natural minor** scale contains **flattened 3rd, 6th and 7th degrees** and you start with the note **C**, you would come up with the following notes –

C, D, E♭, F, G, A♭, B♭, C

If you know that the **harmonic minor** scale contains **flattened 3rd, and 6th degrees**, but a **natural 7th degree**, all you have to do to change the natural minor to the harmonic minor is **sharpen the 7th degree by a semitone**. Once again if you start with the note **C**, you would come up with the following notes –

C, D, E♭, F, G, A♭, B, C

To change the harmonic minor to an **ascending melodic minor** you need to **sharpen the 6th degree by a semitone**. Starting with the note **C**, you would come up with the following notes –

C, D, E♭, F, G, A, B, C

The Classical form of the descending melodic minor is identical to the natural minor. To become familiar with the notes of minor scales in all keys, it is important to **write out the three types of minor scales starting on each of the 12 notes of the chromatic scale**.

The following examples demonstrate melodies created from the three types of minor scales.

 62 Natural Minor Melody

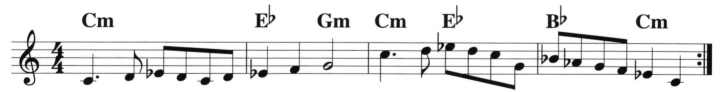

 63 Harmonic Minor Melody

 64 Melodic Minor Melody

It is also important to be able to transpose melodies in minor keys. The process is the same as for major keys – write the scale degrees under the melody notes and then work out what notes those degrees equate to in the key you want to transpose to. Shown below is the previous example transposed to the key of **A minor** with the scale degrees written under the notes.

65   A Melodic Minor

Here is the same example transposed to **F minor**. The key signature of F minor contains **four flats**, but the sixth and seventh degrees of the melodic minor are raised, so the notes **D** and **E** will be **naturals**. Remember to learn the notes of the scale first, then work out the scale degrees.

$$F, G, A\flat, B\flat, C, D\natural, E\natural, F$$

66   F Melodic Minor

TABLE OF MINOR SCALES

Here is a table which shows the notes of the traditional melodic minor scale in all twelve keys. Remember that the **descending melodic minor is the same as the natural minor**. To work out the notes for the **harmonic minor**, simply **flatten the 6th** degree of the ascending melodic minor.

	T	S	T	T	T	S	T	T	S	T	T	S	T		
A MELODIC MINOR	A	B	C	D	E	F♯	G♯	A	G♮	F♮	E	D	C	B	A
E MELODIC MINOR	E	F♯	G	A	B	C♯	D♯	E	D♮	C♮	B	A	G	F♯	E
B MELODIC MINOR	B	C♯	D	E	F♯	G♯	A♯	B	A♮	G♮	F♯	E	D	C♯	B
F♯ MELODIC MINOR	F♯	G♯	A	B	C♯	D♯	E♯	F♯	E♮	D♮	C♯	B	A	G♯	F♯
C♯ MELODIC MINOR	C♯	D♯	E	F♯	G♯	A♯	B♯	C♯	B♮	A♮	G♯	F♯	E	D♯	C♯
G♯ MELODIC MINOR	G♯	A♯	B	C♯	D♯	E♯	G	G♯	F♯	E♮	D♯	C♯	B	A♯	G♯
D♯ MELODIC MINOR	D♯	E♯	F♯	G♯	A♯	B♯	D	D♯	C♯	B♮	A♯	G♯	F♯	E♯	D♯
D MELODIC MINOR	D	E	F	G	A	B♮	C♯	D	C♮	B♭	A	G	F	E	D
G MELODIC MINOR	G	A	B♭	C	D	E♮	F♯	G	F♮	E♭	D	C	B♭	A	G
C MELODIC MINOR	C	D	E♭	F	G	A♮	B♮	C	B♭	A♭	G	F	E♭	D	C
F MELODIC MINOR	F	G	A♭	B♭	C	D♮	E♮	F	E♭	D♭	C	B♭	A♭	G	F
B♭ MELODIC MINOR	B♭	C	D♭	E♭	F	G♮	A♮	B♭	A♭	G♭	F	E♭	D♭	C	B♭
E♭ MELODIC MINOR	E♭	F	G♭	A♭	B♭	C♮	D♮	E♭	D♭	C♭	B♭	A♭	G♭	F	E♭
ROMAN NUMERALS	Ī	IĪ	IIĪ	IV̄	V̄	VĪ	VIĪ	VIIĪ	VIĪ	VĪ	V̄	IV̄	IIĪ	IĪ	Ī

To finish things off, here is a great piece by **J.S. Bach** from Sonata number 2 for flute and harpsichord. On the recording it is played by flute and piano. It is written in the key of **G minor** in ⅜ time. There are many great pieces written for other instruments which can also be played on the harmonica. Look for Classical flute or clarinet pieces and also Jazz saxophone solos. Keep playing, keep practicing and play with other musicians as often as possible.

67 Siciliano

J.S. Bach

JAM ALONG PROGRESSIONS

Congratulations on finishing the book! By now you should be sounding very good and be getting a lot of pleasure from your harmonica playing. To add to that pleasure, and help you practice everything you have learned, there are some extra tracks which have been recorded for you to jam along with. Try out any of the licks in the book with these progressions, and make a habit of improvising your own licks and solos. As well as this, you should play with other musicians as much as possible, as this will help to develop your playing and also put your licks in a musical context.

 68 12 Bar Blues Shuffle in G

 69 Slow Blues in G (With Stops)

 70 Country Rock in G

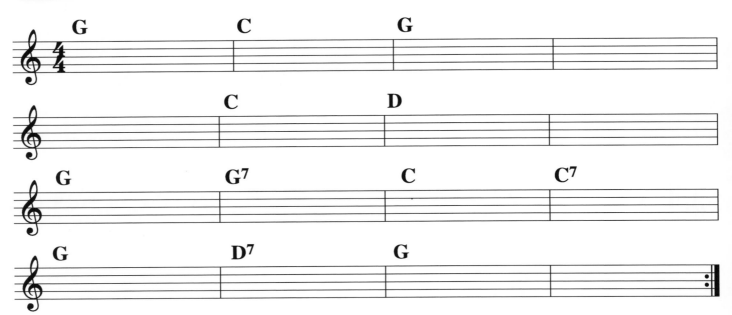

 71 Blues in D Minor

 72 C Major/A minor Jam-Along

PERFORMING IN PUBLIC

Performing in public can be both exciting and frightening for any new performer whether they are an instrumentalist, a singer, an actor or simply someone giving a speech on a social occasion. Many people who are shy at first develop into dynamic performers who can both entertain and captivate an audience. Like any other skill, performing in public takes time to develop and there is much to be learned from watching other performers. To begin with, the best approach can be to simply take a deep breath, walk on, smile, look the audience in the eye and begin with a song you are very familiar with. If you are nervous, concentrate on the sound you and your accompanist(s) are making and move your body to the music in any way that feels good. If you are able to enjoy yourself, this will communicate itself to the audience. Nervousness can be turned into excitement and positive energy and can actually make your natural reactions and responses to the music quicker.

OVERCOMING NERVES

There are three essential elements in overcoming nervousness and turning it into a positive. The first of these is **knowing your material well**. This means thoroughly rehearsing all aspects of each song before you even consider performing them. If you are unsure of the key or which harp to use, or the notes or timing of either the melody or the accompaniment, it is not surprising that you would become nervous. The more certain you are of these things, the more you are free to concentrate on expressing the meaning and feeling of each song and making great music.

The second element is **being comfortable with your equipment and your environment**. Most public performances involve the use of microphones. Using a microphone is discussed on page 61. When you are on stage, it is important to be comfortable using the microphone and to not be startled by hearing yourself through the PA system or foldback speakers. If possible, it is advisable to have a sound check before members of the public arrive. Most professional ensembles have a thorough sound check in which all the equipment is tested individually and together at least an hour (preferably more) before the show. This allows everybody to become comfortable with the sound of the room as well as the equipment. If you learn a bit about PA systems you can also communicate your requirements and preferences to the person operating the sound system.

The third element is **trusting yourself**. If you are considering playing in public, you are probably fairly confident that you are making a good sound when you play and you have probably received compliments from friends as well. In this case, you should be able to play equally well or better in public, particularly once an audience begins to respond. Your body instinctively knows every aspect of producing a good sound, so it is usually just a case of "letting go" and becoming part of the music. The more you can become the character in each song (like an actor) the more convincing your performance will be and the better you will be able to deliver it.

EYE CONTACT

When you play music, you are telling a story to the audience. Look at them as you tell this story and they will respond. Obviously you cannot look at everybody, but you can pick out certain people (e.g. someone wearing bright clothing or someone with a bald spot on their head). Another option is to look towards the people in the middle of the audience. Change your focus from time to time to include all sections of the audience. Everybody will feel you are communicating with them personally and will enjoy your performance more. Remember that when people go to hear a public performance, they are looking forward to having a good time. This means they are automatically prepared to like you even before they see or hear you, so in reality the performance should be a positive experience for everyone involved. Another important aspect of any performance is eye contact between the performers. The fact that an ensemble are communicating well and obviously enjoying themselves makes the audience feel good too.

STAGE PRESENCE AND STAGE CRAFT

Most great performers have what is commonly known as good **stage presence**. Stage presence is the total impression created in the minds and emotions of the audience by the performer(s). This impression is made up of both the drama of the music and speech and the drama of the visual performance. As mentioned earlier, there is much to be learned by watching other performers. It is essential for aspiring performers to see professional musicians, singers, actors or other entertainers perform live as often as possible in the early stages. You can do this by going to shows or by watching performances on video or television. Notice how each performer communicates with both their ensemble and the audience. Learn how they use both spontaneous and choreographed movement. Watch how the music is expressed through their bodies and facial expressions as well as their sound. Notice whether they use humour or not, or any other element of public performance you can think of. All these things can be learned and developed and can be described as the various parts of stage craft.

DEVELOPING YOUR OWN STYLE

Many performers learn their stage craft and their ability to express their vocal or instrumental technique by copying other performers at first and then ultimately adapting what they have learned to form their own unique style and presence. Junior Wells seriously studied Little Walter's style of singing and playing early in his career, but later developed his own intensely personal style which has little in common with Little Walter. This is similar to the way students of visual art are taught to copy the works of masters early in their development. By doing this, the student learns about color, form, design, balance, etc. as well as learning technique. However, this is only the first step in the process. The idea is to master the practical elements in order to be able to go on and express your own feelings, ideas and personality through your own work. Copying a Rembrandt or Picasso painting is an extremely valuable exercise for an art student, but it is not an end in itself. So it is with playing and performing. Learn all you can from performers you admire, whether it is their technique, their musicianship or their stagecraft. Study them in detail and work diligently on everything you learn, particularly in the early stages of your development. However, it is not recommended that you slavishly copy any particular person's style over a long period of time (unless you want to be a comedy act). As your confidence develops along with your personal feelings for the music you are performing, your own style will begin to emerge by itself if you let it. As you practice and perform, notice the things that you feel most intensely about. These are the seeds which will grow into your own vital style if you are true to them and develop them properly.

MICROPHONES

It is essential for all harmonica players to know how to use a microphone. Even if you perform mainly in small rooms with only a guitar or piano accompaniment, it is likely that you will be required to use a microphone at some stage. If you play with a band, you will use a microphone every time you perform. It is a good idea to have your own microphone that you are comfortable with, even if the venue you are performing at provides them along with the PA system.

MICROPHONES FOR PERFORMING LIVE

There are several different types of microphones available. Each of them is best suited to a different musical situation (e.g. live band performance, or recording session).

The type of microphone most commonly used for live performances is the **dynamic microphone**. These microphones contain a diaphragm and a coil which is activated when the voice causes it to vibrate. Dynamic microphones are normally uni-directional, or "front sensitive" which means that sounds entering from the sides of the microphone are amplified less than sound entering from the top or front. Because of their resistance to feedback (the piercing sound made when a microphone picks up the sound coming from the speakers and amplifies it again) uni-directional microphones are particularly useful in a live band environment.

Microphones which are omni-directional receive sound equally from all sides of the microphone. This makes them useful for back-up vocals in situations where two or more singers share one microphone, but they are not recommended for a lead singer in a live band situation.

Before you buy a microphone it is advisable to visit a music store and try out some in the store. The Shure SM58 microphone shown in the photo below is a typical professional quality uni-directional dynamic microphone and is one of the most common microphones used by bands when a clean, natural sound is required. There are also other good microphones available which are of a similar design. If you intend to perform in public regularly, it is worth spending a little extra on a good microphone as it will make you sound better and make you more comfortable with your sound on stage.

Shure SM58 – A Typical Dynamic Microphone

AMPLIFICATION

When playing with a band, it is often necessary to amplify your harmonica. This can be done by using a harmonica microphone such as a Shure "green bullet" (shown below) and plugging it into an amplifier (usually a guitar amplifier) or by playing directly into a vocal microphone through a PA system. It takes practice to play well with amplification, so if possible it is best to rehearse regularly with your amplified sound before playing live.

Although you can easily play with a vocal mic on a stand, it is more common to hold a harp mic in your left hand and control the harp with your right hand when playing amplified. This takes practice and is worth developing at home and in rehearsal before attempting it on stage. You may experience problems with unwanted "feedback" at first. This can be overcome by not standing too close the front of the amp and adjusting the volume and tone knobs on the amp until you get a good strong but controlled sound.

"Green Bullet" Harmonica Microphone

NEALE Valve Amplifier

OVERDRIVE

One of the advantages of using a harp mic such as a green bullet and running it through an amp is that this enables you to get a distorted or "overdriven" sound which sustains more and sounds more electric than a harp played through a vocal mic. Listen to players like Little Walter, Big Walter Horton, James Cotton and Rod Piazza to hear great examples of amplified harp playing. There are no rights or wrongs with amplified playing. It is simply a matter of personal taste.

APPROACH TO PRACTICE

Regardless of the style of music you play, it is important to have a correct approach to practice. You will benefit more from several short practices (e.g. 20-30 minutes per day) than one or two long sessions per week. This is especially so in the early stages, because of the basic nature of the material being studied and also because your lips and facial muscles are still developing. If you want to become a great player you will obviously have to practice more as time goes on, but it is still better to work on new things a bit at a time. Get one small piece of information and learn it well before going on to the next topic. Make sure each new thing you learn is thoroughly worked into your playing. This way you won't forget it, and you can build on everything you learn.

In a practice session you should divide your time evenly between the study of new material and the revision of past work. It is a common mistake for semi-advanced students to practice only the pieces they can already play well. Although this is more enjoyable, it is not a very satisfactory method of practice. You should also try to correct mistakes and experiment with new ideas. It is the author's belief that the guidance of an experienced teacher will be an invaluable aid in your progress. To develop a good feel for timing, it is essential that you always practice with a metronome or a drum machine.

LISTENING

Apart from books, your most important source of information as a musician will be recordings. Listen to albums which feature harp players. Some important Blues players to look out for are: Sonny Terry, Little Walter, Sonny Boy Williamson, Junior Wells, Big Walter Horton, James Cotton, George "Harmonica" Smith, Billy Branch, Paul Butterfield, Snooky Pryor, Jerry Portnoy, Sugar Blue, Charlie Musselwhite and Rod Piazza.

For Country, Folk and Rock playing, listen to Charlie McCoy, Brendan Power, as well as the simple but effective playing of Neil Young and Bob Dylan. Some of the best **Chromatic** harmonica players include Larry Adler, Toots Thielemans, and Stevie Wonder.

There are also numerous great Jazz and Blues sax players who are worth checking out. Little Walter got a lot of his ideas from listening to sax players. Some of the most Bluesy sax players are: Maceo Parker and Pee Wee Ellis (solo or with James Brown) King Curtis, Junior Walker, Fathead Newman, A.C. Reed, Eddie Shaw, Eddie "Cleanhead" Vinson, Scott Page, Illinois Jacquet, Stanley Turrentine, Eddie Harris, Ben Webster, Johnny Hodges, and Roland Kirk who often played two saxophones at a time!

Guitar Players are another good source of ideas. Listen to the guitarist on any Blues album and you will hear note bending, slides, grace notes and other techniques which are equally effective on the harmonica. Some guitarists to look out for are BB King, Otis Rush, Buddy Guy (with Junior Wells or solo), Magic Sam, Lightnin' Hopkins and Albert Collins along with Robert Junior Lockwood and Luther Tucker who can both be found on albums by Sonny Boy Williamson.

When you are listening to albums, try to sing along with the solos and visualize which holes you would play and the techniques you would use to achieve the sounds you are hearing. This helps you absorb the music and before long, it starts to come out in your own playing. It is also valuable to play along with albums, sometimes imitating what you are hearing and other times improvising. This is very good ear training and is also a lot of fun.

TRANSCRIBING

As well as playing along with albums and imitating what you hear, it is important to work out solos and melodies you admire and write them down exactly. This is called **transcribing**. By doing this, you can analyze the player's note choices and rhythmic idiosyncrasies and find out exactly what makes them sound the way they do. By doing this, you will be able to analyze the lines to understand what it is you like about them and then incorporate them into your own playing. It is important to transcribe a variety of players from different eras rather than just imitating one favorite (who wants to be a clone?). You will learn something different from each player and will also open yourself up to new ideas and new sounds.

All the great players have done lots of transcribing. Make it part of your daily practice routine. When you have memorized a new melody or solo, try playing it with a play-along recording of the song it came from or one with a similar progression (e.g. a Blues). Once you can play the solo perfectly, use it as a basis for improvising and then use the ideas you come up with next time you play with other musicians. Make a habit of this and your playing will never stop developing.

RECORDING YOURSELF

From time to time it is a good idea to record your performances or practice sessions. Unless you have studio quality equipment, the tone quality you hear on the recording may not be completely accurate, but any recording will pick up timing and relative pitch accurately. As you listen back to yourself, pay particular attention to areas you think are particularly weak or particularly strong. Anything you think sounds good is worth developing further and anything that doesn't (e.g. timing, or pitching on bent notes) should be the focus of your practice sessions until it is turned into a strength.

LEARNING MORE ABOUT MUSIC

Regardless of your aspirations, your playing will benefit from learning as much about music as you can. By now you should have a good basic understanding of how melody and rhythm works, how beats can be subdivided and what keys are. However, many harmonica players don't know much about chords or harmony (e.g. keyboard or rhythm guitar accompaniment). If you have a basic understanding of these subjects you can contribute much more to band arrangements and songwriting. In fact, it is strongly recommended that you learn at least a bit of general music by taking up bass, guitar or keyboards. Ask the other musicians you play with about what they are doing and get them to show you a few things. Of course, the harmonica will still be your main instrument, but harp players who understand music are always popular and usually get lots of work.